Eggs o Toast

Written by Isabel Thomas

Illustrated by Eva Byrne

Collins

The children are having eggs on toast for lunch.

Preeta starts to tuck in.

I love eggs!

3

But Tarik and Trisha think eggs are too plain.

They start to look for better toppings.

Tarik spoons on some sweetcorn.
Trisha tips ALL the sweetcorn on
her toast!

SPLAT!

Tarik scatters raisins on his toast.
Trisha plonks on all the raisins from the jar!

Tarik grabs a scoop of green jam.

I can munch as much as you!

Tarik drops on three little carrot sticks.
Trisha adds a tower of carrot sticks!

Next, Tarik tips on a blob of brown mustard.

Trisha squeezes out three blobs.

SQUELCH!
SQUELCH!
SQUELCH!

Trisha jumps up on her chair.
She crowns her toast tower with
a packet of crisps!

But then the children get a shock.
Trisha's toast tower starts to tilt.

The food slips down, down, down ...

BUMP!
 THUMP!
  SPLAT!

Tarik groans. Now it's Preeta's turn to boast.

I think I'll stick to eggs on toast.

Lunch

:paw: Review: After reading :paw:

Use your assessment from hearing the children read to choose any GPCs, words or tricky words that need additional practice.

Read 1: Decoding

- Support the children to practise reading two-syllable words.
- Ask the children to:
  - Read the sounds in each syllable "chunk" and blend.
  - Then read each chunk to read the whole word.

child/ren	children	sweet/corn	sweetcorn
scatt/ers	scatters	per/fect	perfect

  - Now read the words quickly without chunking them up.

Read 2: Prosody

- Model reading each page with expression to the children.
- After you have read each page, ask the children to have a go at reading with expression.

Read 3: Comprehension

- Look at pages 14 and 15 together. Ask the children to compare what each of the children have on their menu list, using "more than", "less than", "taller" etc. (e.g. *Tarik has more than Preeta. Preeta has less than Trisha.*)
- For every question ask the children how they know the answer. Ask:
  - How do you think Trisha felt when she finished building her food tower (page 10)? How do you think she felt when the tower fell down (page 12)?
  - What do you think Mum said to Trisha on page 13?
  - What do you think happened next?